Megalithic Art in Ireland

Dr Muiris O'Sullivan

With photographs by John Scarry

Country House, Dublin

Published in 1993 by
Town House and Country House
42 Morehampton Road
Donnybrook
Dublin 4
Ireland

British Library Cataloguing in Publication Data. A catalogue record for this book is available from the British Library.

ISBN: 0-946172-36-6

Illustration acknowledgements
Deborah Gamble, frontispiece, and drawing page 31; Muiris O'Sullivan, plates 1, 17, 19 and 20; The Wiltshire Collection, photo 5, and Jim Bambury, photos 4 and 9, copyright The Office of Public Works, Dublin; Pat Collins, photo 3, copyright Department of the Environment, Northern Ireland; John Delaney, plate 17; Hilary Richardson, drawing page 41. All of the remaining photographs are by John Scarry.

Frontispiece: Decorated basin, eastern tomb, Knowth 1
This basin is situated in the right-hand recess, which, as in many other cruciform tombs, is distinguished architecturally, artistically and ceremonially. Although only a few bear applied ornament, the stone basins are sculptured objects whose occurrence mirrors the distribution of megalithic art in Ireland.

Managing editor: Treasa Coady
Text editor: Séamas Ó Brógáin
Design: Bill Murphy
Origination: The Kulor Centre
Printed in Ireland by Criterion Press, Dublin

CONTENTS

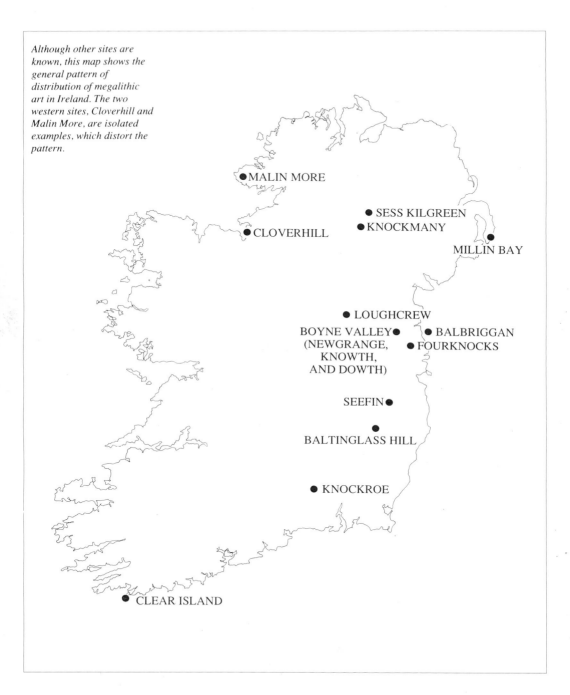

Although other sites are known, this map shows the general pattern of distribution of megalithic art in Ireland. The two western sites, Cloverhill and Malin More, are isolated examples, which distort the pattern.

●MALIN MORE

● SESS KILGREEN
●KNOCKMANY

●CLOVERHILL

MILLIN BAY

● LOUGHCREW

BOYNE VALLEY●   ● BALBRIGGAN
(NEWGRANGE,   ●FOURKNOCKS
KNOWTH,
AND DOWTH)

SEEFIN●

●
BALTINGLASS HILL

● KNOCKROE

● CLEAR ISLAND

'MEGALITHIC ART' refers to an ornamental tradition that flourished along the western edge of Europe during the Late Stone Age and Early Bronze Age. Examples of this art survive on the structural stones of megalithic tombs and on pottery and other portable objects found within them.

These examples are but a tiny sample of the original production, which must have included work on fabric, wood, and other perishable materials. Striking evidence for this turned up in 1991 when the body of a man who lived five thousand years ago emerged from the Alpine snows during an unusual thaw. Tattoos on the body, consisting in this case of simple lines, may have been contemporary with Irish megalithic art.

This art evolved at the end of the Stone Age, coinciding with the spread of agriculture. It seems that agriculture emerged about ten thousand years ago in western Asia. Within a relatively short time farming was being practised in south-eastern Europe, and by 5000 BC it had spread to the western Mediterranean coasts and up the Danube into Germany and France. The earliest farmers in Ireland lived some time around 4000 BC, and Irish megalithic art reached its full bloom about 3000 BC.

MEGALITHIC TOMBS

Along the Atlantic coast of Europe the neolithic (Late Stone Age) and megalithic traditions are often indistinguishable. During the neolithic period, from the Mediterranean in the south to southern Scandinavia in the north, enormous resources were expended in the construction of so-called megalithic tombs. The term is technically accurate but it should not be taken too literally: while burials do indeed occur in these monuments, occasionally in great profusion, it is likely that many of the megalithic sites played a considerably wider role.

A megalithic tomb is an artificial cave built of large stones and usually covered by a mound. The normal practice was to erect the cave using massive slabs or drystone walling covered by lintels or corbelling. Over this skeletal structure was thrown a massive mound of clay or stones. The most common European megalith is the passage-tomb, in which the internal structure consists of a passage leading to a chamber.

It is our good fortune that some neolithic people decorated the megalithic monuments using techniques that enabled the art to survive for our admiration. The usual technique is picking, but engraved ornament occurs also, and in Iberia painting has survived. Megalithic art has a restricted distribution in Europe. The most remarkable concentration is centred on the Boyne Valley in Ireland, and there are other concentrations in western Iberia and around the Golfe du Morbihan near Carnac in Brittany.

Neolithic art also survives in the form of objects placed within the tombs. Large numbers of sculptured objects, interpreted as idols, have been recovered from sites in Portugal and Spain. Decorated pottery was also deposited. In Ireland the cremated remains in passage-tombs are frequently accompanied by beads and pendants carved from semi-precious stones. At prestigious sites like Knowth and Fourknocks in Co Meath, larger carved objects were also included. Not only are the objects carved into specific shapes but surface ornament also occurs on them. The most dramatic example is the ceremonial macehead recovered from a significant position in the eastern tomb at Knowth (Pl 2). It is at Knowth too that the two traditions, structural and portable, merge. The decorated stone basin placed in the right-hand recess of the eastern tomb has the scale but not the function of a structural stone and was clearly deposited for ceremonial purposes (Frontispiece).

IRISH PASSAGE-TOMBS

Passage-tombs, especially in Ireland, are the classic repositories of megalithic art. These monuments are a relatively standard element of the neolithic tradition in continental Europe, but in Ireland they seem to stand slightly aloof from the common neolithic tradition. In the archaeological record this aloofness revolves around ceremonial, ornamental and architectural features, but it may in practice have extended to issues such as life-style, belief systems, and sources of wealth.

The mound covering a passage-tomb is more or less round and is generally retained at the edge by a kerb of boulders (Pl 14). This kerb is a uniquely Irish feature, and it is significant that some of the more innovative examples of megalithic art in Europe occur on kerbstones in the Boyne Valley. In general, however, the art occurs in the interior of the tombs, mainly on the structural stones of the passage and especially the chamber. Many of the chambers in the Irish passage-tomb tradition were built on a cruciform plan, with recesses at each side and at the rear. The right-hand recess was often distinguished structurally and ritually. It is not surprising, therefore, that particularly impressive ornament occurs in the right-hand recess of the more ambitious structures in the Boyne Valley and on the hills at Loughcrew, Co Meath.

An exact count of Irish passage-tombs is difficult to provide. This is because unopened hilltop cairns need not necessarily belong to this class of monument. However, a minimum of about one hundred and fifty is acceptable, and the total could be twice this figure. Megalithic art occurs in about fifty passage-tombs and on stones from some other sites whose relationship to the passage-tomb tradition is unclear.

Most of the decorated sites, accounting for more than four-fifths of the decorated stones, are in Co Meath. These lie close to the River Boyne and its

Photo 1 Decorated passage-tomb, Seefin, Co Wicklow
Mountain summits were a favoured location. It is clear that the obvious practical difficulties of building at this height were a lesser consideration than the symbolic message to be conveyed by the prominent siting.

9

tributary the Blackwater. Apart from these, decorated passage-tombs occur in central and eastern Ulster and in a loose distribution extending southwards across the mountains from Dublin to the foothills of Slievenamon on the Kilkenny-Tipperary border. There is also a significant cluster of decorated sites on the other side of the Irish Sea, on the island of Anglesey and close to the Mersey before it reaches Liverpool. Isolated examples include a decorated stone from Clear Island, Co Cork, and a disputed site at Cloverhill on the verge of the Carrowmore cemetery in Co Sligo.

ORIGINS OF IRISH MEGALITHIC ART

Scholars have argued about the origins of Irish megalithic art, but few accounts have attempted to trace the tradition from infancy to old age.

Its immediate origins are uncertain. The earliest manifestations relied on a small repertoire of basic geometric elements. Parallels for this repertoire can be cited in western Iberia, mainly in megalithic tombs but also, in the case of the spiral, on living rock in the countryside. These themes, however, are mingled with other motifs that do not appear in Ireland. This seems to preclude a direct transfer from Iberia to Ireland, against which there are other objections too.

It is likely that behind the Irish and Iberian traditions of megalithic art there lies a deeper ornamental pool from which both drew inspiration. In the earlier neolithic cultures of south-eastern Europe, from about 6500 BC onwards, various objects were decorated using a repertoire that included the ornamental elements that emerged later as the common denominator between Irish and Iberian art. This earlier tradition is probably ancestral to both the Irish and the Iberian ornament, whatever their relationship to each other.

It is unlikely that megalithic art arrived in Ireland as a package that had been assembled elsewhere. A more likely explanation is that Irish megalithic art evolved parallel to its European cousins under the influence of contemporary traditions rooted further east. In its earliest form it was considerably closer to Iberia than to Brittany, but to search for a point of origin anywhere on the Atlantic coast of Europe would be to oversimplify a complex situation. Remarkably, it was at a more mature stage in each case that the megalithic art of Ireland, Brittany and Iberia showed its greatest convergence.

SEQUENCE OF STYLES

In megalithic art, individual sites have their distinctive styles; however, there is a standard insular style that occurs throughout the distribution of megalithic art, not just in Ireland but also in Britain.

Photo 2 Kerbstone 59, Knowth 1, Co Meath
Detail showing a standard piece of native Irish passage-tomb art. The ornamentation was usually applied by picking, but the artists' tools have not been recognised. Neither have any concentrations of waste chipping come to attention.

Standard examples of megalithic art in Ireland are based on a small range of basic elements that are varied and sometimes combined in a manner whose logic is not fully understood (Photo 2). Sometimes the individual elements are organised into neat two-dimensional compositions, but more frequently they are applied in a way that from the point of view of visual design seems haphazard. Apart from the fact that overlapping motifs frequently occur, there are instances, even where conditions of preservation have been favourable, in which the motifs are difficult to distinguish. In addition, the art frequently occurs on surfaces that became hidden as soon as the structures were completed. It is as if

11

the process of applying these motifs, or perhaps their presence on the stones, was more important than their visual impact. Obviously this possibility has a significant bearing on any discussion of the meaning of the ornament.

This standard idiom occurs throughout Irish megalithic art, in the Boyne Valley and elsewhere. However, in the great tumuli at Knowth, Newgrange and Dowth another style is also present. By contrast with the standard style it displays a remarkable sympathy for the configuration of the surface on which it occurs (Pl 6). Because of this sculptural quality it is termed a 'plastic' style. This style aspires towards visual grandeur and was apparently created to enhance the architectural impact of the structure.

In sequence, the plastic art is secondary to the standard art. It overlies the standard art on certain surfaces and, more remarkably, usually displays a disregard for the presence of the previously existing elements: it simply cuts through them, without taking the trouble either to avoid them or to remove them completely. It never occurs on a hidden or inaccessible surface, which suggests that it was applied after the structures had been completed. Although some of the finest pieces of this plastic art, such as the Newgrange entrance stone (Pl 7), used standard motifs, there was a tendency to move away from these elements and to create designs that were inspired primarily by the shape of the stones (Photo 5). This more mature ornament was developed in an environment of contact with megalithic societies on the shores of the Golfe du Morbihan and possibly at the mouth of the Tejo (Tagus) in Portugal.

These overseas influences are best seen within the tombs at Knowth, Newgrange, Dowth, and Fourknocks. However, it is on the kerbstones in the Boyne Valley that the most ambitious innovations occurred, as it was here that the mature style was based not on overseas borrowings alone but on a blend in which the native elements were prominent; hence the retention of native elements in the great kerb designs at Newgrange (Pl 8) and Knowth.

DECLINE IN CREATIVITY

The blanket-picking that marks the ultimate development of megalithic art in the Boyne Valley left little room for further development. The decline in creative energy is summed up at Millin Bay, Co Down, by a seemingly late

Photo 3 Stone M20, Millin Bay, Co Down
The crook-like device on this stone is a Breton feature, but the Millin Bay art is more generally a provincial version of the developed Boyne style.

structure where the art mixes features of the developed plastic style with intrusive elements from Brittany without ever managing to achieve a coherent design (Photo 3). Millin Bay is unorthodox in many ways, and the rules are broken elsewhere too. Megalithic art was incorporated in unusual structures at Lyle's Hill, Co Antrim, and Cloverhill, Co Sligo. The rock art of Early Bronze Age Scotland occasionally incorporated elements that would have been more at home in megalithic art. The overlap between megalithic art and rock art in Ireland deserves further study, but there is little evidence that megalithic art contributed significantly to the subsequent tradition.

THE BOYNE VALLEY

The River Boyne seems to have played a major role in the ceremonial life of the passage-tomb people. A remarkable scatter of mounds, many of them still unopened, lies near the river. The great mounds at Knowth, Newgrange and

13

Dowth overlook the bend of the Boyne from the highest ridges in the area. These three cairns and their immediate satellites contain more than six hundred decorated stones, an enormous gallery that surpasses the known total for Brittany and Iberia combined.

Knowth

More than three hundred decorated stones occur in the large tumulus at Knowth (known as Knowth 1), the greatest concentration by far of megalithic art in Europe. Nearly eighty pieces of decorated stone occur elsewhere on the site, more than half of them in the associated satellites and the remaining fragments in various displaced locations.

The potential artistic wealth at Knowth was first brought to light in modern times by Prof R A S Macalister, who conducted a small investigation in 1941, but the credit for systematically revealing this great assemblage of megalithic art goes to Prof George Eogan, who has been directing excavations at the site since 1962.

The decorated kerb of the large tumulus must have been regarded as a remarkable achievement in its time. Although a few gaps occur, it is likely to have consisted of one hundred and twenty-seven kerbstones, of which about ninety are decorated. Of these about seven-tenths bear ordered compositions, many having large-scale designs of magnificent simplicity in a version of the plastic style. The curve of the kerb flattens out along the eastern and western sides of the tumulus, and the longest kerbstone in each case lies opposite the entrance stone. The art on the northern side of the kerb is the least imposing; elsewhere, however, a steady proportion of the designs are impressive and innovative.

A survey of eighty-five of the decorated kerbstones reveals that they can be grouped according to design features. For example, the main theme on thirteen of the kerbstones is a dominant circular device (Pl 4); on nine others it is a large serpentiform motif (Photo 7); and on a further seventeen it is an arrangement built up using separate circles and spirals (Photo 6).

Whatever the reason for these individual themes, the overall production marks the emergence of a remarkable school of art, emphasising grandeur of scale, boldness of expression, and simplicity of design. A desire for visual

14

cont. p 17

Photo 4 Stone settings along the western façade, Knowth 1, Co Meath
These settings remind us that the artwork is only one of the symbolic features in passage-tombs. Water-rolled pebbles and fractured quartz, sometimes transported from distant sources, are also found along the façades.

15

Photo 5 Kerbstone 74, Knowth 1, Co Meath
*Abandoning the traditional motifs of Irish passage-tomb art, the artist capitalised on the
stone's outline as an inspiration for the design. The vertical slash in the middle reminds us that
the entrance to the western tomb lies behind this kerbstone.*

Photo 6 Kerbstone 56, Knowth 1, Co Meath
*Example of an artwork in which a combination of circles and/or spirals produces an integrated
design. Here the artist deployed the traditional geometric elements according to a new
aesthetic canon. This design faces site 4, a prestigious satellite of the main mound.*

16

Pl 1 Unopened cairn, Slievenamon, Co Tipperary
There is insufficient evidence to describe this unopened site as a passage-tomb, but it is well to remember that the cairn lies within view of Knockroe, a decorated megalith. The natural rock formation on the eastern side may have served as a false entrance.

impact, not always a feature of megalithic art, was clearly an important factor in many cases. There was innovation too in the treatment of the stone itself: many of the designs reflect the outline of the stone or seem to be influenced by the configuration of its surface (Photo 5). What we are seeing here is the emergence of the plastic style.

Art of a less imposing character, in the standard Irish passage-tomb style, is also found. It is the exclusive style on the backs of kerbstones, and when it occurs on the fronts it is sometimes overlaid by the new style.

A similar blend of more and less innovative ornamentation occurs within the tombs. What may be termed standard megalithic art occurs with some frequency on the fronts, sides and backs of structural stones; it is distributed throughout the passages and chambers and even on the corbels and lintels of the roof.

A more dramatic style occurs on the fronts of some orthostats clustered in the passages at the approach to the chambers. Artistically the designs can only be fully understood in the context of the stones on which they occur. This is particularly evident in the case of the famous anthropomorphic design on

17

cont. p 21

Photo 7 Kerbstone 57, Knowth 1, Co Meath
Example of a sprawling serpentiform design, and typical of the kerb art at Knowth. Laudable efforts are now being made to preserve the freshness of the picking, but a professional programme of conservation is urgently required.

Photo 8 Kerbstone 86, Knowth 1, Co Meath
Apart from the ribbon-picking, which produces a flat and bland effect, there are also some incised motifs on the surface of this stone.

18

Photo 9 Orthostat 49, western tomb, Knowth 1, Co Meath
This face-like design guards the entrance to the chamber. Parallels occur in Brittany, often similarly located within the structure. The seemingly effortless symbiosis between material, design and imagery is a mark of genius. Standard geometric elements have been abandoned in favour of a sculptural approach.

19

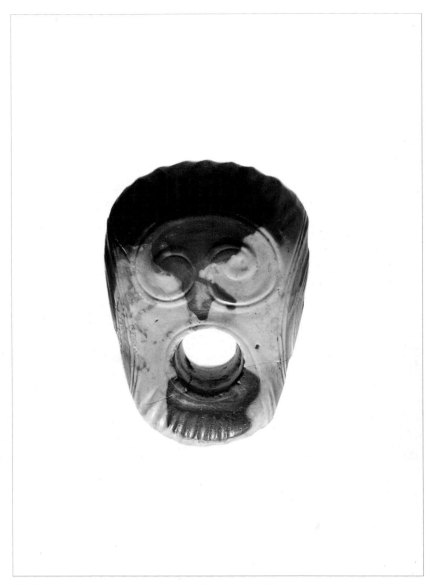

Pl 2 Decorated macehead, eastern tomb, Knowth 1, Co Meath
Ceremonial object found at the entrance to the right-hand recess. The spectacle-spirals remind us of the macehead's British background; the face-like appearance is reminiscent of the Iberian idols; but the unique blend of form, decoration and symbolism may be a Boyne contribution. (Printed in actual size.)

Pl 3 Kerbstone 15, Knowth 1, Co Meath
This is the most spectacular image of the 'sun-splash', a motif that occurs at Newgrange, Loughcrew, and elsewhere at Knowth. Does it represent a sun-dial? In this case the 'sun-splash' is rotated slightly clockwise to accommodate the design on the right.

Pl 4 Kerbstone 51, Knowth 1, Co Meath
Example of an artwork dominated by a prominent circular field of ornament. This feature recurs on a number of kerbstones at Knowth. Notice that the large design, which was obviously added later, respects the outline of the spiral on the left. This is an unusual gesture, but it is not unique.

Pl 5 Kerbstone 52, Knowth 1, Co Meath
The more extensive later arrangement, which shows little concern for the pre-existing spiral in the middle, was applied with reference to the profile of the stone. Serpents and circles are standard elements in Irish megalithic art.

Pl 6 Kerbstone 88, Knowth 1, Co Meath
A fine example of the plastic style, this design would make little sense if separated from the shape of the particular stone on which it occurs.

orthostat 49 in the western tomb (Photo 9), but it is a feature that can be observed on most of the stones in the series. While the concentration of these designs is found at the point where the chamber begins to evolve from the passage,

21

both the backstone and the entrance kerbstone in each tomb are also decorated in the same style. A few further examples are found elsewhere in the chambers.

There is a clear distinction between these special designs and the remaining ornamentation of the tombs. The special designs never occur on inaccessible surfaces. They sometimes overlie the more general ornament, and their scale, plasticity and conscious visual impact set them apart. The implication is that they were added when the structure was in place, a view that is supported by the fact that these designs never extend fully to ground level. By contrast, the original style must have been in vogue when the structures were being built. The original art was based faithfully on the standard geometric elements, whereas, as if to emphasise its separateness, the superimposed art ranged considerably beyond this system.

Megalithic art has been recorded on twelve of the satellite mounds surrounding the large tumulus at Knowth. With a few exceptions, the designs in the satellites are in the less ambitious standard idiom.

Newgrange

The art on the famous entrance stone at Newgrange is probably the finest integrated design in megalithic ornament (Pl 7). By decorating the convex surface with a large curvilinear arrangement, the artist has made the stone itself look considerably more massive than it is. Another ambitious composition occurs on Kerbstone 52 (Pl 8). The art on Kerbstone 67 is almost as distinguished (Photo 10). Overall, however, the ornamentation of the Newgrange kerb does not match the sustained grandeur achieved at Knowth. Of the kerbstones at Newgrange exposed by Prof Michael J O'Kelly's excavations from 1962 to 1975 and by the less extensive work completed by the Office of Public Works in more recent times, art occurs on about seven-tenths. Apart from the three stones mentioned above and a few other examples at the entrance, the kerb is decorated in a standard Irish passage-tomb style.

Standard ornamentation is also to be found on the stones within the tomb. Spectacular examples include the roofstone of the right-hand recess (Pl 11), the famous triple-spiral design in the end recess (which, incidentally, is composed of six spirals) (Pl 9), and the mysterious 'face' on orthostat L19 in the passage (Pl 10).

However, it is within the Newgrange tomb that the most extreme expression of the plastic style occurs. It is so extreme that the O'Kelly excavation team

Photo 10 Kerbstone 67, Newgrange, Co Meath
The false-relief design on the left contrasts both in technique and rhythm with the flowing S-spiral on the right. The result is dramatic. This is one of the three masterpieces that enable Newgrange to stand comparison with the Knowth kerb.

regarded it as 'pick-dressing', which they differentiated from art in the normal sense (Pl 9). But this exclusion was based on a traditional understanding of megalithic art in which the individual elements were seen as paramount. It is now clear that the pick-dressing or blanket-picking is a developed version of the plastic style, in which the focus seems to have shifted entirely from the motifs to the stone itself. There is a sense of artistic loss in this extreme development: the moment of greatness has passed. This blanket-picking is found on every one of the passage orthostats, on some of the chamber orthostats, and on the kerbstones at the entrance. On the entrance stone it extends over the great curvilinear design and, like that design, fades out towards an imaginary horizontal line near ground level (Pl 7).

The blanket-picking at Newgrange, like all the plastic art in the Boyne Valley, invariably occurs on accessible surfaces, and it overlies the existing art wherever the two occur together. (A notable exception is orthostat L19 (Pl 10),

23

cont. p 26

Pl 7 Kerbstone 1 (entrance stone), Newgrange, Co Meath
Since the art runs out near ground level, it is suspected to have been applied in situ. *The plastic quality of the design, a superlative work of art, makes the stone look deceptively rotund.*

Pl 8 Kerbstone 52, Newgrange, Co Meath
Positioned directly across the mound from the entrance stone, this striking plastic design is the work of a genius who drew inspiration from the stone's awkward contours.

Pl 9 Orthostat C10, Newgrange, Co Meath
In all there are six spirals in this arrangement, but it is popularly known as a triple spiral. It is often borrowed as a symbol of ancient Celtic spirituality, although we have no evidence that it was ever seen by a Celt until the seventeenth century AD. An area of blanket-picking spreads along the surface nearby.

Pl 10 Orthostat L19, Newgrange, Co Meath
Visitors pass this design at the point where the chamber begins to open from the passage. The pre-existing ornament was left carefully untouched by the artist applying the blanket-picking, suggesting that the earlier design was still sacred. Many see it as a schematic face, possibly a deity.

Pl 11 Roofstone, right-hand recess, Newgrange, Co Meath
This piece, based on standard elements, was locked into the structure during the construction phase. The location of this attractive design in the right-hand recess, where special features are characteristically assembled, reminds us that the meaning of passage-tomb art is a complex issue.

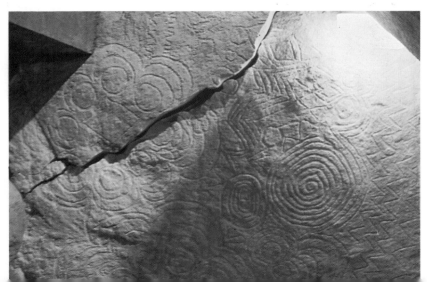

where the creator of the secondary ornament was careful to avoid impinging on the 'face' design.) As at Knowth, the plastic ornament tends to follow the configuration of the surface and to focus towards the side that is visible to a person approaching the stone from the entrance.

At least three satellite tombs are known in the immediate vicinity of Newgrange. Excavations have revealed a total of nineteen decorated stones, which, as in the Knowth satellites, are in the standard Irish style.

Photo 11 C19, northern tomb, Dowth, Co Meath
This is the most profusely decorated stone in the tomb. The arrangement of radiating lines, focused on the edge of the stone and superimposed on other motifs, shows an emerging interest in the form of the stone itself.

Dowth

Although less well known than that of Newgrange and Knowth, the art at Dowth displays the same general stylistic characteristics. Based on what is known from earlier excavations, it seems that a mixture of standard passage-tomb art and impressive large-scale designs like those on the Knowth kerb remain to be discovered along the Dowth kerb. The few kerbstones that are still visible on the eastern side of the mound are in line with this view.

As at the other two sites, the standard Irish passage-tomb art was followed by the plastic style. Both styles can be seen in the recess of the southern tomb at Dowth and in various parts of the cruciform northern tomb (Photo 11). As at Newgrange and Knowth, the plastic style occurs most frequently along the passage.

The blend of genius and international influences that drove the Boyne Valley artists to dizzying heights of creativity was not repeated on a large scale elsewhere in Ireland. A few individual sites, such as Fourknocks (although this is not in the Boyne Valley), seem to have participated in this creative spirit. But

Loughcrew was largely untouched by the changing attitudes, and we find little trace of the developed style there.

FOURKNOCKS

Unusually for an Irish site, this passage-tomb has no megalithic kerb. But the chamber contains a spectacular array of decorated stones, including one — the first orthostat on the left side of the chamber — that may be a stylised anthropomorphic image (Pl 12).

The finest pieces occur on the lintels overlying the entrances to the end and right-hand recesses (Pl 13), but other remarkable pieces were found in the general area of the entrance passage. In general the Fourknocks art forms neat patterns. Where the surface is flat, as in the lintels, the ornament is rectilinear, and where the surface is convex the ornament is curvilinear. This is a typical

Photo 12 Fourknocks, Co Meath
This mound is brilliantly restored. Sensitively placed shaft-holes funnel the natural light onto the decorated surfaces in the chamber within the mound.

27

Pl 12 Orthostat C1, Fourknocks, Co Meath
This is an ambiguous image, a schematic representation of a face and torso with a suggestion of limbs and possibly a belt. It is an Irish version of a theme that was then current in France and Iberia. The image always appears in or near the chamber.

Pl 13 Stone E, Fourknocks, Co Meath
Fields of angular ornament are associated with the entrance to the recesses at Fourknocks,
Newgrange, and Knowth. The design results from wedding an Iberian regularity to a
traditional Irish motif. A native version of this design occurs in cairn T, Loughcrew.

feature of the plastic style. One stone, found overlying the orthostats on the left
side of the entrance passage, resembles the Newgrange entrance stone in its
overall design, but otherwise the Fourknocks art is almost unique. Because the
art is so obviously organised into linear patterns, comparisons with the 'idol' art
of Iberia have been mentioned.

29

LOUGHCREW

About one hundred and twenty decorated stones have been found at Loughcrew, although the original figure is likely to have been considerably greater. The vast majority of these occur in two clusters of tombs, a group on one summit (Carnbane West) focusing on cairn L and another group (Carnbane East) focusing on cairn T. The Loughcrew art did not share in the spectacular innovations that led to the mature plastic style in the Boyne Valley. It is essentially a standard collection of Irish megalithic art in which the motifs are frequently crowded onto the surfaces in a busy and seemingly unfocused manner (Pl 15). But it also features some exquisite designs. The arrangement on the backstone of cairn T, for instance, is a neatly balanced piece of composition (Pl 16). There are strong indications that this and some other stones, especially in cairn T, were decorated after being placed in position, but it is clear that other pieces of ornament were applied before construction and then locked into inaccessible locations.

The Loughcrew art was first brought to public attention in the 1860s. At that time a series of reliable illustrations was prepared by the artist du Noyer. By the end of the nineteenth century the megalithic art at Loughcrew was seen to be suffering from the elements. Its original impact is difficult to envisage now, especially on exposed surfaces. Nevertheless we can appreciate from du Noyer's drawings and the surviving evidence that many of the designs must have been impressive in their pristine state.

Some years ago Dr Elizabeth Shee-Twohig made a fresh recording of the Loughcrew ornament. Subsequently, around 1980, a Japanese expedition used a sophisticated rubbing technique to construct their own record of the Loughcrew ornament, but this, sadly, remains unpublished.

THE NORTHERN SITES

Two remarkable structures lie within a few kilometres of each other near Ballygawley, Co Tyrone. The art at Sess Kilgreen would be relatively unremarkable were it not for the extraordinary design on one of the backstones (see drawing opposite). This arrangement is often interpreted as an owl-like

Orthostat C6, Sess Kilgreen, Co Tyrone
This design, sometimes speculatively interpreted as an owl-like goddess of death, peers from a stone that squats at the back of the chamber. With its neighbour on orthostat C5 it stands apart from the standard designs at Sess Kilgreen and throughout Ulster.

face. In general the Sess Kilgreen art is restrained (single motifs are the norm on each stone). By contrast the nearby Knockmany tomb features an exuberant proliferation of motifs, which have the same busy appearance as the Loughcrew ornament.

In the northern part of Ireland there are a number of decorated stones whose precise context in relation to megalithic art is difficult to define. A strange assemblage of stones, decorated in an advanced plastic style, was found in an intriguing structure on the shore at Millin Bay, Co Down. At Cloverhill, Co Sligo, another strange tomb carries ornament that is so distinctive its validity as

31

Pl 14 Cairn T, Loughcrew, Co Meath

Passage-tombs are normally enclosed by cairns that are edged with megalithic kerbstones. This is one of the focal sites at Loughcrew, and it contains several decorated stones.

Pl 15 Orthostat C16, cairn L, Loughcrew, Co Meath

This is the backstone of the right-hand recess in a cairn that is the focus of the decorated sites on Carnbane West. The art is crowded and some of the elements overlap, which is a rare occurrence at Loughcrew.

32

megalithic art has been questioned (Pl 21). At Malin More, Co Donegal, decoration occurs, uniquely, in a court-tomb.

These exceptions suggest that the orthodoxy of the passage-tomb tradition wavered in the northern part of Ireland. The evidence from south-west Scotland bears out this view. Rock art, a separate tradition from megalithic art in Ireland and Britain, occurs in some profusion in Argyll. Apart from the standard rock art motifs, such as circles and cupmarks, some of the Argyll surfaces carry motifs that belong exclusively to the passage-tomb tradition. Similarly, passage-tomb motifs occur on a stone circle at Temple Wood and on slabs from cist graves of the earlier Bronze Age in south-west Scotland. The overall impression is that cross-fertilisation took place between the passage-tomb tradition and some of the incoming earlier Bronze Age cultures in this joint Hiberno-Scottish province.

KNOCKROE

Until recently it was customary to cite Baltinglass Hill, Co Wicklow, as the most southern example of a decorated passage-tomb. (The stray decorated stone from Clear Island, Co Cork, was regarded as the exception that proved the rule.) During the 1980s, however, a local antiquary, Johnny Maher, brought Knockroe, Co Kilkenny, to the attention of archaeologists. In scale it is a modest site compared with the focal cairns of the Boyne and Loughcrew, but it seems to have had an importance beyond its size. Like Newgrange, where the impact of the rising sun on Midwinter's Day is so well documented, it has a solar alignment. In Knockroe, however, it is to the setting sun on Midwinter's Day that the western tomb is directed (Pl 18).

Some of the decorated surfaces at Knockroe, especially along the kerb, have suffered badly from the effects of weathering, but the chamber ornament is in good condition, and elsewhere the art can be seen in optimum light. Every kerbstone examined on the southern side of the cairn was found to be decorated, but no kerbstone on the northern side had any art. It is on the northern side of the Knowth kerb too that art is poorly represented. Comparisons with Knowth do not end there, because one of the Knockroe kerbstones has an arrangement of snake-like lines, a typical Knowth design (Pl 19). The eastern tomb has not been

33

Pl 16 Orthostat C8, cairn T, Loughcrew, Co Meath
Although aesthetically pleasing, this is standard passage-tomb art, lacking the sculptural awareness of the developed Boyne Valley style. The attractive flower-like elements recur elsewhere at Loughcrew.

unearthed at the time of writing, but the western tomb is heavily decorated. The ornament seems to aspire towards the mature style. On two stones facing each other across the chamber, comprehensive designs extend over the entire face (Pl 20).

Pl 17 Decorated stone, Knockroe, Co Kilkenny
This stone was found lying on its decorated face near the eastern tomb. It may have been a
lintel or an orthostat.

BEYOND IRELAND

The distribution of megalithic art in Ireland is heavily focused towards the Irish
Sea. Crossing that sea, therefore, it is not surprising to find megalithic art on the
island of Anglesey and along the Mersey near Liverpool. There is also a link
with the megalithic art of the Orkney Islands. The seagoing tradition reflected in
these links brought the island megalithic art into contact with the continental
centres in Brittany and Iberia.

35

WHAT DOES MEGALITHIC ART MEAN?

The literature concerning the meaning of passage-tomb art tells us more about the authors than about the artists. This is not surprising, because symbols are empty in themselves: it is the people looking at them who invest them with meaning, which is related to their personal interests and the information at their disposal. For this reason, the convinced interpreter is unreliable.

In earlier centuries, some commentators perceived the art as ancient linguistic symbols, which they tried to compare with known scripts. Others preferred interpretations linking the art with astronomical phenomena. By the first half of the twentieth century, originating in a brilliant paper by the French archaeologist Déchelette, it was common to see abstract human faces in the designs — and in a few cases the illustrations were distorted to emphasise the point. There followed a reactionary period, especially during the 1970s, when the meaning of the ornament became less of an obsession, giving way to an analysis of technique and basic content. Nevertheless the question on the lips of the general public is still, 'What does it mean?' Enter pseudo-science to fill the vacuum.

The pseudo-scientific literature, especially that of the 1980s, draws heavily on archaeological research but is frequently almost paranoid about archaeologists. Prehistorians, for their part, find it difficult to cope with the claims of science fiction, which, operating according to different principles, has no difficulty in leaping chasms of logic.

In the pseudo-scientific literature, specific decorated stones are examined out of context, and the art is given interpretations that are modern-day variations on the eighteenth-century calendrical and astronomical themes. The various solutions to the so-called code are backed up by mathematical formulations, scientific-looking diagrams, and dramatic photographs. The solutions are attractive, the illustrations convincing, and the mathematical formulations too complicated for most people to bother about. Unfortunately this literature tells us little about the meaning of megalithic art. On the contrary, because it perceives the ornament narrowly as essentially a pseudo-mathematical code, it diminishes the background and sophisticated achievements of Stone Age people.

The cultural context

The motifs constituting the vocabulary of Irish megalithic art did not suddenly appear from nowhere. The early agricultural communities of central and south-eastern Europe were using these elements thousands of years before they appeared in megalithic art. As research continues, it begins to emerge that the meaning of Irish passage-tomb art cannot be considered without reference to its symbolism in this original pool.

Apart from that consideration, however, it is misleading to consider the overall meaning of the art without reference to the full spectrum of symbolic features in passage-tombs, and not just a favoured few. It is generally acknowledged that the structures are not merely a reflection of ancient burial customs. They provide clues to the attitudes and life-style of their designers. The siting of certain monuments in relation to observed astronomical features indicates that such features had a special significance. However, the tendency to give additional prominence to the right-hand side in cruciform structures is a feature deserving equal attention. Entrance features in the form of kerb modifications and stone settings, internal features like sillstones, roof modifications, and stone basins, the burial rite and associated grave goods — all these, and much more, are part of the symbolism of passage-tombs. The art too can provide information about the culture of the passage-tomb people. Interpreted narrowly, however, it can distort our understanding.

We have already traced the evolution of megalithic art from a straightforward depictive style to a compositionally more sophisticated plastic style. At its most extreme, this involved a shift in emphasis from the individual decorative element, such as a spiral or triangle, to the structural stone itself. Leaving aside all other considerations, our search for the meaning of the art should take this shift into consideration. It is remarkable that the geometric elements inherited from earlier times, presumably laden with deep symbolism, were rapidly made redundant.

Rehabilitating the anthropomorphs

The stylistic developments identified in the Boyne Valley can also be traced in Brittany. The later megalithic art of Brittany and also of Iberia is full of anthropomorphic symbolism. Designs that look like abstract faces and torsos are

37

cont. p 40

Pl 18 Winter solstice, Knockroe, Co Kilkenny
On Midwinter's Day the setting sun reaches the south-western horizon at a point that is directly in line with the passage of the western tomb. The cyclical life of nature is a recurring theme in Stone Age symbolism, reflecting a holistic spirituality rooted in the natural environment.

38

Pl 19 Decorated kerbstone, Knockroe, Co Kilkenny
The serpentiform arrangement shows the artist's awareness of themes that otherwise in Ireland only occur at Knowth, although they are also found in Brittany and Iberia. A systematic programme of conservation is required to prevent these ancient works of art from weathering into oblivion.

Pl 20 Decorated orthostat, western tomb, Knockroe, Co Kilkenny
The art in the western tomb at Knockroe shows a number of remarkable similarities with the ornament in the famous site on the island of Gavrinis, Brittany.

39

prominent, often in symbolically critical locations within the structure. Naturally formed stones having an anthropomorphic appearance were sometimes appropriated and enhanced.

In Ireland the anthropomorphic images emerge more clearly in the developed style. At Newgrange the face-like design on orthostat L19 at the approach to the chamber (Pl 10), which has close parallels in the portable ornament of Iberian megalithic tombs, is carefully avoided by the overlying plastic ornament. The famous anthropomorphic design on orthostat 49 in the western tomb at Knowth confronts the visitor at a similar juncture (Photo 9). Designs of a remarkably similar nature occur in similar positions in Brittany. The Knowth macehead, an overtly anthropomorphic image (Pl 2), occurs at the entrance to the especially favoured right-hand recess. This design is assembled in a manner that can be closely paralleled on the famous cylinder idols of Iberia. And of course there is the cartoon-like figure in the chamber at Fourknocks (Pl 12).

Who is the figure being represented? An attractive theory promulgated by Marija Gimbutas suggests that it is an image deriving from the Great Goddess, seen as the pre-eminent deity of ancient Europe before the arrival of the Indo-Europeans. We must make our own judgements on this.

The suggested presence of a few anthropomorphic images among the designs does not mean that all or even a large body of megalithic art has to do with anthropomorphism. Prof Eogan has shown that certain design packages tend to recur in the same part of various tombs. These arrangements show no obvious anthropomorphic features, but the pattern of recurrence emphasises that they were important symbolically in the context of the structures.

One kerbstone at Knowth bears a spectacular design that, on examination, is no more than a developed version of a motif repeated at Newgrange, Loughcrew, and even on other stones at Knowth itself (Pl 3). The elements of this motif are so distinctive that its repetition cannot be accidental. Some have suggested that it may be a sundial. They may be right. This is a case where a relationship with solar observations could be explored.

Any discussion of this topic faces the difficulty that some of the examples were built into places where they were hidden from the sun. This reminds us that hidden ornament is an important feature of megalithic art, a dimension that requires consideration in the context of symbolism.

40

cont. p 44

A drawing of the art on the Knowth macehead. (See Pl 2.)

Pl 21 Cloverhill, Co Sligo
Lying apart at the edge of the Carrowmore group, Cloverhill is a strange piece of passage-tomb architecture. Its art is equally unusual, and many scholars attribute it to the Iron Age. However, most of its elements recur elsewhere in megalithic art, especially in marginal sites.

Pl 22 (facing page) The Balbriggan stone, Co Dublin
This stone was found recently on the seashore near Balbriggan. Art or a natural accident? Although many passage-tombs survive in the area, none of them is known to be decorated. However, Fourknocks, a highly decorated structure, lies a few miles inland.

42

These few probes are not the last word on the meaning of megalithic art. Rather they are intended as a beginning, suggesting avenues that might be explored. All lines of enquiry, as long as they are followed with due deference to the evidence, are valid. Contrary to the claims of science fiction, there is no simple code that will explain the sophisticated symbolism of the art, any more than knowing the Hindi word for a cow could tell anyone what a cow means to a Hindu. The symbolism will continue to intrigue future generations, but in the meantime the important question may not so much be what it means intrinsically as what it means to each individual.

44

GLOSSARY

anthropomorph: a conventionalised representation of the human form.

blanket-picking: a technique by which a considerable area of the stone's surface is removed (sometimes described as 'pick-dressing').

corbelling: a roofing technique used in passage-tombs in which stones (corbels) projecting slightly out from the wall support the weight overhead.

incision: a technique whereby the motifs were cut into the surface using a sharp burin or chisel, leaving a fine line that can only be seen in exceptional lighting conditions.

lintel: a stone spanning the distance between two supporting uprights such as a pair of jambstones or orthostats.

orthostats: boulders standing on end to act as the wall of a megalithic tomb.

pick-dressing: *see* 'blanket-picking'.

picking: the technique found most frequently in megalithic art, in which a sharp stone was used to peck at the surface and thus create the classic picked effect.

plastic art: an art term, used here to describe a developed style of megalithic art in Ireland, in which the ornament is moulded into the shape and configuration of the stone.

quartz: a crystalline rock, usually white or off-white in colour, which is often found in the cairns of passage-tombs and which sparkles brightly immediately after being drenched by rain; traditionally considered to have special properties.

ribbon-picking: a form of blanket-picking found at Knowth in which the motifs are delineated by a flat ribbon of picking.

solstice: the time when the sun reaches its maximum distance from the equator, in effect the longest and shortest days of the year, 21 June and 21 December, respectively.

standard art: the original Irish style of passage-tomb art, in which basic geometric elements were depicted on a surface, with little reference to the plastic qualities of the stone itself.

45

SELECT BIBLIOGRAPHY

Almagro Gorbea, Maria Jose, 'Los ídolos del Bronce I Hispano', *Bibliotheca Praehistorica Hispana,* vol 12 (1973).

Eogan, George, *Knowth and the Passage-Tombs of Ireland,* Thames and Hudson, London, 1986.

Gimbutas, Marija, *The Language of the Goddess,* Harper and Row, San Francisco, 1989.

Herity, Michael, *Irish Passage Graves,* Irish University Press, Dublin, 1974.

Le Roux, Charles-Tanguy, 'A propos des fouilles de Gavrinis (Morbihan): nouvelles données sur l'art mégalithique Armoricain', *Bulletin de la Société Préhistorique Française,* vol 81, 240–45.

O'Kelly, Claire, 'Passage-grave art in the Boyne Valley', *Proceedings of the Prehistoric Society,* vol 39 (1973), 354–82.

O'Kelly, Michael J, *Newgrange: Archaeology, Art and Legend,* Thames and Hudson, London, 1982.

O'Sullivan, Muiris, 'Approaches to passage tomb art', *Journal of the Royal Society of Antiquaries of Ireland,* vol 116 (1986), 68–83.

— 'The art of the passage tomb at Knockroe, County Kilkenny', *Journal of the Royal Society of Antiquaries of Ireland,* vol 117 (1987), 84–95.

— 'A stylistic evolution in the megalithic art of the Boyne Valley', *Archaeology Ireland,* vol 3, no 4 (winter 1989), 138–42.

— 'The transformation in the passage tomb art of western Europe', *Journal of Indo-European Studies,* vol 19 (spring-summer 1991), 15–27.

Shee-Twohig, Elizabeth, *The Megalithic Art of Western Europe,* Clarendon Press, Oxford, 1981.